Credits

President & CEO	Robert Darbelnet
Executive Vice President, Publishing & Administration	Rick Rinner
Managing Director, Travel Information	Bob Hopkins
Director, Product Development	Bill Wood
Director, Sales & Marketing	John Coerper
Director, Purchasing & Corporate Services	Becky Barrett
Director, Business Development	Gary Sisco
Director, Tourism Information Development	Michael Petrone
Director, Travel Information	Jeff Zimmerman
Director, Publishing Operations	Susan Sears
Director, GIS/Cartography	Jan Coyne
Director, Publishing/GIS Systems & Development	Ramin Kalhor
Product Manager	Beverly Donovan
Managing Editor	Margaret Cavanaugh
Development Editor	Greg Weekes
Marketing Manager	Bart Peluso
AAA Travel Store & E-store Manager	Sharon Edwards
Manager, Business Line Publicity	Janie Graziani
Print Buyer	Laura Cox

Book production by Vinings Publishing

Editor	Mark D. Shekerow
Writer	JoAnn Polley
Photography	Photodisc, Inc.
Design	Infinite Ideas & Designs, Inc.

Copyright © 2002 AAA Publishing. All rights reserved.

Published by AAA Publishing
1000 AAA Drive, Heathrow, Florida 32746

Printed in the USA by Quebecor World

ISBN 1-56251-803-8   Stock Number: 204402

For information about other titles published by AAA, visit our e-store at www.aaa.com

No part of this book may be reproduced in any form or by any electronic or mechanical means, including information storage and retrieval devices or systems, without prior written permission from the Publisher, except that brief passages may be quoted for reviews. The contents of this book are believed to be correct at the time of printing. The publisher is not responsible for changes that occur after publication.

TABLE of CONTENTS

North American Map 4, 5
Acadia National Park 6
Biscayne National Park 7
Chequamegon National Forest 8
Cherokee National Forest 9
Everglades National Park 10
Great Smoky Mountains
   National Park 11
Hot Springs National Park 12
Ouachita National Forest 13
Isle Royale National Park 14
Mammoth Cave National Park . . .15
Daniel Boone National Forest 16
Shenandoah National Park 17
George Washington National
   Forest 18
Jefferson National Forest 19
Arches National Park 20
Big Bend National Park 21
Bryce Canyon National Park 22
Dixie National Forest 23
Canyonlands National Park 24
Capital Reef National Park 25
Carlsbad Caverns National Park . .26
Lincoln National Forest 27
Mesa Verde National Park 28
San Juan National Forest 29
Grand Canyon National
   Park 30, 31
Great Basin National Park 32
Lehman Caves National Park 33
Petrified Forest National Park 34
Saguaro National Park 35
Zion National Park 36
Death Valley National Park 37
Joshua Tree National Park 38

Inyo National Forest 39
Sequoia & Kings Canyon
   National Park 40, 41
Yosemite National Park 42, 43
Sierra National Forest 44
Badlands National Park 45
Black Canyon of the Gunnison
   National Park 46
Bridger-Teton National Forest 47
Grand Teton National Park 48, 49
Rocky Mountain National
   Park 50, 51
Roosevelt National Park 52, 53
Waterton/Glacier National
   Park 54, 55
Lewis & Clark National
   Forest 56, 57
Shoshone National Forest 57
Yellowstone National Park 58, 59
Targhee National Forest 60
Crater Lake National Park 61
Lassen Volcanic National Park . . .62
Lassen National Forest 63
Mount Ranier National Park . . .64, 65
Gifford Pinchot National Forest . .66
North Cascades National Park . . .67
Mount Baker/Snoqualmie
   National Park 68
Olympic National Forest 69
Olympic National Park 70, 71
Redwood National Park 72
Six Rivers National Forest 73
Denali National Park 74
Tongass National Forest 75
Parks & Forest Crossword 76
Wacky Parks Story 77
Index 78–80

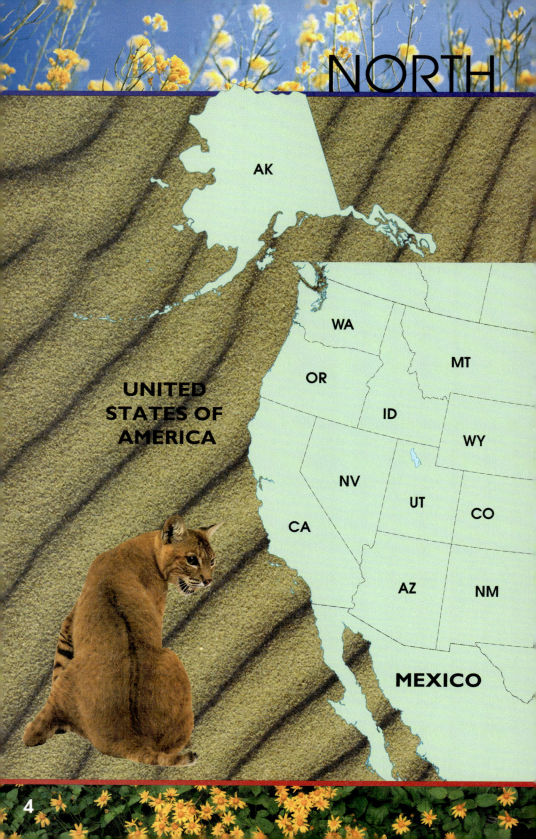

ACADIA national park

Named L'Isle des Monts in 1604 and in 1916 re-named Lafayette National Park, it received its current name, Acadia, in 1929. Archaeological evidence indicates the presence of American Indians around 6,000 years ago, and geological evidence suggests that Desert Island was actually formed some 20,000 years ago by floods from melting glaciers! As the nation's fifth smallest park at 47,633 acres, it is one of the top 10 visited with over 3 million visitors a year. You'll encounter a diverse landscape filled with numerous ponds, 26 mountains, 40 different kinds of mammals and over 273 species of birds alone. One thing you should try to do while you're here is hike up to the top of Cadillac Mountain (1,530 feet) for an extraordinary view of the sunrise.

DAY I VISITED

THE WEATHER WAS

THE FIRST THING I NOTICED WAS

I DIDN'T EXPECT TO SEE

THE COLORS OF THE PARK ARE

THE NEATEST THING I SAW WAS

MY FAVORITE PART OF ACADIA WAS

ONE THING I WILL TELL MY FRIENDS IS

I WOULD/WOULDN'T LIKE TO COME BACK BECAUSE

MAINE

BISCAYNE national park

The history of this park includes British, French, and Dutch pirates who used to prowl the vicinity of the park attempting to rob Spanish fleets carrying valuables back to Spain! In 1980, President Jimmy Carter designated this watery wilderness a national park. Here you not only can snorkel, swim, scuba, and sail, but you land-lubbers can also take a glass-bottom boat to see the ocean's lush corals and schools of vibrantly colored fish. You can also hike along various self-guided nature trails filled with colonies of herons, egrets, ibis, and pelicans. Hike along Mangrove Shore and you may even see a peregrine falcon or a bald eagle. In the wintertime, look closely and you might spot the endangered sea cow, the manatee!

DAY I VISITED

THE WEATHER WAS

THE WATER WAS

THE FIRST THING I DID WAS

THE MOST AMAZING THING I SAW WAS

THE NEATEST PART OF THE PARK WAS

THE BIRDS I GOT TO SEE WERE

ONE THING I WILL TELL MY FRIENDS ABOUT IS

I WILL ALWAYS REMEMBER

FLORIDA

CHEQUAMEGON
national forest

Experience the serenity that comes with over 850,000 acres of lush forests, sparkling streams, and rushing rivers. Established as a national forest in 1933, Chequamegon, pronounced sho-WAH-ma-gon, means place of shallow water. Named by the Ojibwa tribe, it has a rich history of fur traders, loggers, missionaries, and American Indians. It is Wisconsin's largest national forest. Try your hand at fishing in the 632 miles of rivers and streams for walleye, bass, and trout. Go bird-watching or hike along its more than 200 miles of winding trails filled thick with maple, balsam, spruce, and pine, where you'll come across ruffled grouse, white-tailed deer, and even an occasional black bear!

DAY I VISITED

THE WEATHER WAS

THE FIRST THING I SAW WAS

FOR RELAXATION I

I REALLY ENJOYED

THE ANIMALS I SAW WERE

THE PRETTIEST THING I SAW WAS

THE NEATEST THING THAT HAPPENED WAS

I WILL ALWAYS REMEMBER

WISCONSIN

CHEROKEE national forest

This 635,000-acre forest is the largest tract of public land in Tennessee. Taking its name from the Cherokee Indians, it stretches along the state's eastern border from Chattanooga to Bristol, in the heart of the southern Appalachian mountain range and adjoining the Great Smoky Mountains National Park. Each year millions of people visit this forest to admire its incredible beauty filled with densely wooded pines, hardwoods, and mountain laurels. Some of the mountain peaks soar over 5,000 feet! Geologists estimate that the Appalachians date to 500 million years ago, and that the range was once higher than the Rocky Mountains and the Alps! So enjoy the cold water streams, whitewater rivers, and hundreds of miles of hiking trails, as you enter a forest of tranquility.

DAY I VISITED

THE WEATHER WAS

THE FIRST THING I NOTICED WAS

THE MOST BEAUTIFUL THING I SAW WAS

THE NEATEST ANIMAL I SAW WAS

I REALLY ENJOYED

ONE THING I GOT TO DO WAS

I WILL ALWAYS REMEMBER

I WILL TELL MY FRIENDS ABOUT

TENNESSEE

EVERGLADES
national park

On Dec. 6, 1947 President Harry S. Truman dedicated this park with the words, "Here is a land, tranquil in its quiet beauty, serving not as the source of water, but as the receiver of it. To its natural abundance we owe the spectacular plant and animal life that distinguishes this place from all others in our country." Since then, this lush park has enthralled its visitors with its incredible floral diversity offering over 25 varieties of orchids, and over 1,000 other kinds of seed-bearing plants. The park also has over 36 threatened or endangered animal species, such as the American alligator, crocodiles, the Florida panther, and if you go at the right time, the manatee! And if you fancy birds, keep your eyes open for warbler, falcons, bobolinks, and swallows.

DAY I VISITED _____

THE WEATHER WAS _____

THE FIRST THING I NOTICED WAS _____

THE PARK REMINDED ME OF _____

THE NEATEST THING I DID WAS _____

THE MOST EXCITING ANIMALS I SAW WERE _____

I WAS SURPRISED TO LEARN THAT _____

ONE THING I WILL TELL MY FRIENDS IS _____

I WOULD/WOULDN'T RETURN BECAUSE _____

FLORIDA

GREAT SMOKY MOUNTAINS national park

Since Sept. 2, 1940, when President Franklin D. Roosevelt officially dedicated this park, it has become one of the top ten visited parks in the nation. Its 521,621 acres boasts over 4,000 species of plants, 65 different kinds of mammals, and more than 230 species of birds! You can experience five different forest types. They are the spruce-fir, the northern hardwood, the pine-oak, the hemlock, and the cove hardwood. And each elevation of 1,000 feet is equivalent to moving 250 miles north. So the higher you go, the cooler it becomes. While you may not get a glimpse of the wild European boar, you'll see plenty of red and gray squirrels, deer everywhere, as well as an occasional black bear!

DAY I VISITED

THE WEATHER WAS

THE FIRST THING I NOTICED WAS

I DIDN'T EXPECT TO SEE

I THOUGHT THE TREES WERE

SOME ANIMALS I SAW WERE

MY FAVORITE PART OF THE PARK WAS

ONE THING I WILL TELL MY FRIENDS IS

I WOULD/WOULDN'T LIKE TO COME BACK BECAUSE

TENNESSEE

HOT SPRINGS
national park

When you visit this park you are actually visiting a city of sorts. This park, established March 4, 1921, offers you hot baths from spring waters that flow from Hot Springs Mountain. In the middle of the 19th century, Hot Springs prospered as a health spa, and people came from all over seeking relief from various health afflictions. At the Fordyce Bathhouse you'll see where patrons partook of the luxurious ritual of hot baths. At the Buckstaff Bathhouse you can experience an actual hot springs bath just like they did in the early 1900s. You can also explore various trails and nearby woodlands rich in hickory, dogwood, pine, and redbud. In the springtime, the scenery comes alive with bright wildflowers, roses, and irises!

DAY I VISITED

THE WEATHER WAS

THE FIRST THING I NOTICED WAS

THE TOWN REMINDED ME OF

I REALLY ENJOYED SEEING

I WAS SURPRISED TO LEARN

THE BATHS REMINDED ME OF

I WILL TELL MY FRIENDS ABOUT

THE BEST PART OF THE VISIT WAS

ARKANSAS

OUACHITA national forest

Ouachita (WASH-i-taw) is the French spelling of the Indian word Washita, which means "good hunting grounds." As the South's oldest national forest, its 1,700,000+ rugged, mountainous acres run east and west, rather than north and south as do most American ranges. In addition, novaculite, which is highly valued for making Arkansas whetstones, is plentiful in the area. You'll also find lakes, springs, waterfalls, and the Ouachita River surrounded by a dense pine forest. If weather permits, you can go swimming, boating, and fishing. You can also hike, bike, horseback ride, or just take a breathtaking drive along the 54 miles of the Talimena Scenic Byway, where you'll see a spectacular mountainous view as you cross from Arkansas into Oklahoma.

DAY I VISITED

THE WEATHER WAS

THE FIRST THING I SAW WAS

THE FIRST THING I DID WAS

MY FAVORITE PART OF THE DAY WAS

THE MOST BEAUTIFUL THING I SAW WAS

ONE THING I'D LIKE TO DO AGAIN IS

I WILL ALWAYS REMEMBER

I WILL TELL MY FRIENDS ABOUT

ARKANSAS

ISLE ROYALE national park

This isolated wilderness park offers a complex and untamed environment, rich with grazing wildlife and rugged terrain. Authorized as a national park in 1931, it offers one of the most exhilarating opportunities to experience nature at its finest. The main island, around 45 miles long and nine miles wide, is only accessible by boat or seaplane. Once there, you'll learn about low-impact hiking to preserve the environment. While the trails may be somewhat rough at times, you will be rewarded with frequent exposure to the various wildlife such as moose, beaver, otter, and foxes, who have become accustomed to human presence, and therefore won't run when they see you!

DAY I VISITED

THE WEATHER WAS

WE GOT TO THE ISLAND BY

I WAS SURPRISED TO LEARN

THE FIRST THING I SAW WAS

THE BEST THING THAT HAPPENED WAS

ONE THING I WILL ALWAYS REMEMBER IS

I WOULD/WOULDN'T LIKE TO COME BACK BECAUSE

MICHIGAN

MAMMOTH CAVE
national park

Mammoth Cave, established as a national park on July 1, 1941, has the world's largest known cave system. Over 350 miles of underground passages have been mapped out on five levels, and geologists speculate there could still be 600 miles of undiscovered passageways! As you wind your way down into the cave, keep your eyes open as you look for the more than 200 species of animals. Bats, frogs, crickets, and troglophiles (cave lovers) such as crayfish. Salamanders and spiders live here. You might even see some eyeless fish! Outside, the 52,700 acres contain white-tailed deer, foxes, woodchucks, and all kinds of birds, including mourning doves, hawks, and wild turkeys.

DAY I VISITED

THE WEATHER WAS

THE FIRST THING I NOTICED WAS

INSIDE THE CAVE I FELT

THE COOLEST THING I SAW WAS

I WAS SURPRISED TO LEARN THAT

I LIKE/DON'T LIKE SPELUNKING BECAUSE

ONE THING I'LL TELL MY FRIENDS IS

THE BEST PART WAS WHEN

KENTUCKY

DANIEL BOONE national forest

These impressive 690,000+ acres of rugged mountain country offers spectacular sights, such as 80 natural sandstone arches and cliffs in the Red River Gorge. Formed some 70 million years ago by wind and water, these natural formations of balancing rocks and tabletops will astound you. As you hike the forest as Daniel Boone did many years ago, you'll see chestnut, hickory, beech, red and white oak trees, and over 100 different species of birds, from Canada geese to wild turkeys, loons, and herons. There are 46 kinds of mammals including wild mink and muskrat. Be sure to visit Cumberland Falls, with its 68-foot drop. Legend has it that on the nights of the full moon, you can actually see a "moonbeam" around the falls.

DAY I VISITED

THE WEATHER WAS

THE FIRST THING I NOTICED WAS

I WONDER IF DANIEL BOONE SAW

SOME ANIMALS I SAW WERE

I THOUGHT THE NATURAL ARCHES WERE

THE NEATEST THING I SAW WAS

ONE THING I'LL TELL MY FRIENDS IS

I WILL ALWAYS REMEMBER

KENTUCKY

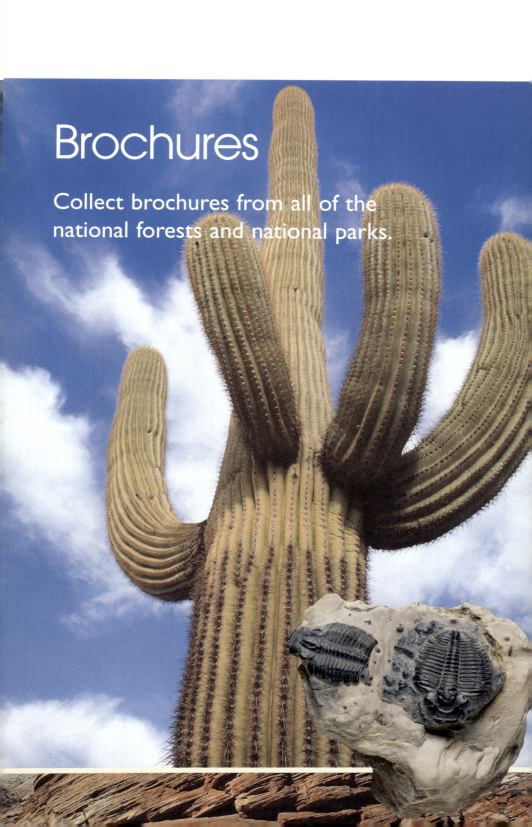

Brochures

Collect brochures from all of the national forests and national parks.

SHENANDOAH national park

Fully established as a national park in 1935, Shenandoah may have gotten its name from the river that runs through it. Of its 196,000+ acres, 79,579 of them are designated wilderness area. This means that those acres are protected so they can retain their natural wild state. So on those trails that pass through this area, you can experience the park's true character. There you'll come across deer, bear, bobcat, wild turkeys, owls, and woodpeckers. You'll see wonderful wildflowers, towering trees, and the mesmerizing peaks of the Blue Ridge Mountains. Hike the Appalachian Trail that runs roughly the length of the park, or just drive along the 105 miles of Skyline Drive to absorb the magnificent panorama of the true Shenandoah.

DAY I VISITED _____

THE WEATHER WAS _____

THE FIRST THING I NOTICED WAS _____

WHEN I SAW THE MOUNTAINS I FELT _____

SOME ANIMALS I GOT TO SEE WERE _____

ONE THING WE DID IN THE PARK WAS _____

THE NEATEST THING WE DID WAS _____

I REALLY ENJOYED _____

THE BEST PART WAS WHEN _____

VIRGINIA

GEORGE WASHINGTON
national forest

This scenic forest extends more than 1,000,000 acres across the Blue Ridge, Massanutten, Shenandoah, and Allegheny Mountains. You can hike more than 950 miles of scenic trails leading to spectacular views of mountains, valleys, and rivers. Part of the 57 miles of the Appalachian Trail leads to Crabtree Falls, which consists of five cascading waterfalls with a vertical drop of over 1,500 feet. As you traverse the forest you'll encounter some of the over 200 species of birds, 55 species of mammals, and over 2,000 species of shrubs and herbaceous plants! From hemlocks to blankets of rhododendron, whether you hike or just take a leisurely drive along the mountainous roads, you'll experience the breathtaking beauty of nature.

DAY I VISITED _____

THE WEATHER WAS _____

WE SAW THE FOREST BY _____

THE FIRST THING I NOTICED WAS _____

WHEN I SAW THE MOUNTAINS I FELT _____

THE PRETTIEST THING I SAW WAS _____

THE ANIMALS I SAW WERE _____

THE BEST PART OF THE VISIT WAS _____

I WILL ALWAYS REMEMBER _____

VIRGINIA

JEFFERSON national forest

In 1995 the George Washington National Forest and Jefferson National Forest were administratively joined as sister forests. Together, they contain nearly 1.8 million acres of public land. Over 700,000 acres are in this forest with 300 miles of the Appalachian Trail running through it. Here you have more than 500 miles of trout streams, six fishing and four swimming lakes, and more than 1,100 miles of hiking trails that you can see by walking or by horseback. If you feel up to a four-mile hike, take the Cascades National Recreation Trail that leads to a 66-foot waterfall. Along the way you will see wonderful wildflowers, and up above you may spot broad-winged hawks circling in the sky!

DAY I VISITED

THE WEATHER WAS

THE WAY I SAW THE PARK WAS

THE FIRST THING I NOTICED WAS

THE ANIMALS I SAW WERE

THE PRETTIEST PART OF THE PARK WAS

THE BEST THING THAT HAPPENED WAS

I WILL TELL MY FRIENDS ABOUT

ONE NEAT THING I DID WAS

VIRGINIA

ARCHES national park

Although in 1929 President Herbert Hoover set aside Arches as a national monument, it wasn't until 1971 that President Richard Nixon officially made it a national park. Geologists attribute millions of years of exposure to water, ice, extreme temperatures, and underground salt movement with the formation of the more than 2,000 natural arches that fill the park. These amazing arches range in size from a three-foot opening to Landscape Arch, which measures 306 feet from base to base! Although the land seems invincible, it isn't. Its fragile ecosystem, called Cryptobiotic Crust, a covering of lichen, algae, and fungi that protects against erosion can easily be destroyed. So step carefully as you visit this mesmerizing place.

DAY I VISITED

THE WEATHER WAS

THE FIRST THING I SAW WAS

WHEN I SAW THE ARCHES I FELT

I WAS SURPRISED TO LEARN

THE NEATEST THING I DID WAS

THE ONE THING I WOULD TELL MY FRIENDS IS

I WILL ALWAYS REMEMBER

I WOULD/WOULDN'T COME BACK BECAUSE

UTAH

BIG BEND national park

Named after the U-shaped bend of the Rio Grande bordering the park, Big Bend offers a wild and rugged Texas wilderness. Established in 1944 by President Franklin D. Roosevelt, this park offers mountain and desert scenery on its 801,000+ acres. You'll find three river canyons, including Santa Elena, whose cliffs rise 1,513 feet above the river and where in 1971 the fossilized bones of a winged pterosaur, with a wing span of 38 feet, were found! As you visit the park you'll come across some of the more than 1,000 types of plants and over 400 species of birds. And as you make your way through this remarkable topographical terrain, the scenery and wildlife will seem more typical of Mexico than of the United States.

DAY I VISITED

THE WEATHER WAS

THE FIRST THING I DID WAS

THE MOST AMAZING THING TO ME WAS

I REALLY ENJOYED SEEING

SOME ANIMALS I SAW WERE

ONE THING I WILL TELL MY FRIENDS IS

I WILL ALWAYS REMEMBER

I WOULD/WOULDN'T RETURN BECAUSE

TEXAS

BRYCE CANYON
national park

Established in 1928, this national park is named after one of the horseshoe-shaped amphitheaters carved on the eastern edge of the Paunsaugunt Plateau. For millions of years, slow-moving or standing water has been eroding these rocks mechanically and chemically, leaving behind an extraordinarily mysterious looking terrain. The rock spires, or pillars, known as hoodoos, offer a fantastic array of sizes and shapes, imbued with a mixture of orange and yellows. A scenic drive to Fairyland Point will reveal one of the most colorful and wildest vistas in the park. Take the short hike down the path to get a real sense of the magical feeling of this amazing place.

DAY I VISITED

THE WEATHER WAS

THE FIRST THING I NOTICED WAS

I THOUGHT THE HOODOOS LOOKED

WHAT AMAZED ME MOST WAS

THE TERRAIN REMINDED ME OF

THE BEST THING I DID WAS

ONE THING I'LL TELL MY FRIENDS IS

I WILL ALWAYS REMEMBER

UTAH

DIXIE national forest

Covering almost 2 million acres, this forest stretches 170 miles across southern Utah. Since its elevations vary from 2,800 feet to 11,322 feet, you can experience some climatic extremes all in one day. The higher altitudes generally get around 40 inches of precipitation, most of which falls as snow, except in July and August, when heavy thunderstorms are common. Here you'll encounter aspen, pine, spruce, and fir. At the lower elevations, summer temperatures can exceed 100° so you'll find the vegetation here much more sparse than at the higher levels. Still, you'll see unusual rock formations, rocky cliffs, and gentle plateaus filled with bobcat, cougar, rabbits, wild turkeys, and even the Utah prairie dog!

DAY I VISITED

THE WEATHER WAS

THE FIRST THING I NOTICED WAS

THE PART WE VISITED WAS

I REALLY ENJOYED SEEING

THE BEST PART OF THE DAY WAS

THE ANIMALS I SAW WERE

I WILL ALWAYS REMEMBER

I WOULD/WOULDN'T COME BACK BECAUSE

UTAH

CANYONLANDS national park

Located in a geologic region called the Colorado Plateau, this breathtaking park was established in 1964 by President Lyndon B. Johnson. Its 337,570 acres consists of thousands of cliffs and canyons, mesas, arches, and spires. The Green River and the Colorado River, which flow together at the heart of the park, carved the two great canyons at the center. At Needles, you'll see remarkable rising spires of sandstone. And in Horseshoe Canyon, you can see Native American rock art believed to date back as far as 1,700 B.C. to A.D. 500. In The Great Gallery there you'll find well-preserved life-size drawings intricately painted in red ocher, some estimated to be 6,000 years old.

DAY I VISITED

THE WEATHER WAS

THE FIRST THING I NOTICED WAS

WE GOT AROUND THE PARK BY

WHEN I SAW THE CANYONS I FELT

THE MOST AMAZING THING I SAW WAS

THE BEST PART OF THE DAY WAS

ONE THING I'LL TELL MY FRIENDS IS

I WOULD/WOULDN'T LIKE TO COME BACK BECAUSE

UTAH

CAPITOL REEF national park

Established in 1971, this park's main geological feature is the 100-hundred-mile long Waterpocket Fold. This awe-inspiring formation resembles a huge wave swelling toward the shore, and graphically illustrates the way the earth's surface developed and eroded. The word "Capitol" in the park's name comes from a colorful part of the wave where the white sandstone formations resemble the U.S. Capitol. These brightly colored tiered cliffs, which rise 1,000 feet above the Fremont River, have basins, or "pockets" that can hold thousands of gallons of rainwater.

DAY I VISITED

THE WEATHER WAS

THE FIRST THING I NOTICED WAS

LOOKING AT THE FOLD MADE ME FEEL

ONE THING I DID HERE WAS

THE ANIMALS I SAW WERE

I WOULD TELL MY FRIENDS ABOUT

I WILL ALWAYS REMEMBER

I WOULD/WOULDN'T RETURN BECAUSE

UTAH

CARLSBAD CAVERNS
national park

Although established as a national park in 1930, it was also designated a World Heritage Site in 1995. This park contains 83 separate caves, including one of the deepest, largest and third longest, chambers in the world. Roughly 250 million years ago, this area lay underneath an inland sea with a horseshoe-shaped reef. Over time, as the sea receded, the reef was buried under thousands of feet of soil. A few million years ago, uplift and erosion began to uncover the reef, and slightly acidic rainwater seeped into the cracks, forming the large underground chambers. As limestone-laden drops fell within the chambers, fabulous formations took place, leaving the extraordinary decorations you see today.

DAY I VISITED

THE WEATHER WAS

THE FIRST THING I DID WAS

WHEN WE WENT INSIDE I FELT

I WAS SURPRISED TO LEARN

THE MOST AMAZING FORMATION WAS

ONE THING I'LL TELL MY FRIENDS IS

I WILL ALWAYS REMEMBER

WHEN WE LEFT I FELT

NEW MEXICO

LINCOLN national forest

This magnificent forest is the home of Smokey Bear, the famous living symbol for the campaign to prevent forest fires. Within the forest are three ranger districts and three major mountain ranges filled with spruce, ponderosa pine, fir, and even some aspen groves. You can go through elevations ranging from 4,440 feet to 11,580 feet, where both vegetation and temperature change as you make your way through the different zones. You'll also see meadows, rock outcroppings, and abundant wildlife, including mule deer, bobcats, coyotes, and black bear.

DAY I VISITED

THE WEATHER WAS

THE FIRST THING I NOTICED WAS

THE AREAS WE WENT WERE

WE GOT THERE BY

THE NEATEST THING I SAW WAS

SOME ANIMALS I SAW WERE

I WAS SURPRISED THAT

THE BEST THING I DID TODAY WAS

NEW MEXICO

MESA VERDE national park

Mesa Verde, Spanish for green table, is one of the nation's major archaeological preserves.

Established in 1906, it consists of more than 4,000 archaeological sites, which include 600 cliff dwellings. Around A.D. 550, the first Ancestral Puebloans (originally referred to as Anasazi by archaeologists) settled here. They lived in subterranean pithouses until around A.D. 750. Then, in the year 1200, they built masonry houses and mesa-topped pueblos. For reasons unknown, they then moved into the alcoves and built cliff dwellings, until they left near the end of the century. Today you can visit some of these alcoves and cliff dwellings where you can get a real feel for how these ancient people lived.

DAY I VISITED

THE WEATHER WAS

THE FIRST THING I NOTICED WAS

I WAS SURPRISED TO LEARN

WHEN I SAW THE CLIFF DWELLINGS I THOUGHT

I WOULD GUESS THE PUEBLOANS LEFT BECAUSE

THE NEATEST THING I DID WAS

ONE THING I WILL TELL MY FRIENDS IS

I WILL ALWAYS REMEMBER

COLORADO

SAN JUAN national forest

This beautiful forest encompassing 1,881,586 acres offers vegetation ranging from high alpine forest to low arid desert. Depending on where you wander you'll encounter mountains, canyons, waterfalls, lakes, rivers, archaeological sites, and unusual landforms at elevations ranging from 6,800 feet to 14,246 feet. Take a horseback ride through the wilderness area. Nearly 300 species of birds inhabit this forest, including the bald eagle, peregrine falcon, and the tiny hummingbird. You'll also come across black bear, elk, bighorn sheep, and if you're lucky, you might even spot a cougar or mountain lion.

DAY I VISITED

THE WEATHER WAS

THE FIRST THING I NOTICED WAS

THE PRETTIEST PART OF THE FOREST WAS

WE TRAVELED THROUGH THE FOREST BY

SOME ANIMALS I SAW WERE

THE NEATEST THING THAT HAPPENED WAS

ONE THING I'LL TELL MY FRIENDS IS

I WOULD/WOULDN'T COME BACK BECAUSE

COLORADO

GRAND CANYON

One of the most spectacular sights anywhere on earth awaits your eyes at this amazing national park. Over 1,000,000 acres greet you, with the Grand Canyon extending 277 miles as the Colorado River roars through it, beginning at Lees Ferry and ending at Grand Wash Cliffs. The width and the depth of the canyon vary from place to place, with the widest running 18 miles and the deepest part 6,000 vertical feet. The rocks of the canyon reveal a complex geologic history. The walls of the canyon range from 550 to 250 million years old, while at the bottom of the canyon, some rocks are as old as 2 billion years! Scientists feel the canyon was formed in the last 5 million to 6 million years by the erosion of the Colorado River, as well as erosion from melting snow and tributary streams, which continues even today.

DAY I VISITED _____

THE WEATHER WAS _____
_____

THE FIRST THING I NOTICED WAS _____
_____

I DIDN'T EXPECT TO SEE _____
_____

WHEN I LOOKED DOWN THE CANYON
I FELT _____
_____

THE MOST AMAZING THING TO ME IS _____
_____

I WAS SURPRISED TO LEARN _____
_____
_____

ONE THING I WILL TELL MY FRIENDS IS _____
_____

THE BEST PART OF TODAY WAS _____
_____

national park

The Grand Canyon National Park has over 300 species of birds, 75 species of mammals, 50 species of reptiles and amphibians, and 25 species of fish. You can go horseback riding, mule riding, hiking, or rafting. During your visit you might spot some mule deer, a bobcat, even a mountain lion! And listen carefully for the sound of the canyon's "pink" rattler along the trail. Up in the sky look for peregrine falcons and impressive bald eagles. On the ground you'll see all kinds of yucca, cactus, and prickly pears, so be sure to wear your socks!

DAY I VISITED

THE WEATHER WAS

TODAY I WENT TO SEE

SOME ANIMALS I SAW WERE

THE BEST PART OF THE DAY WAS

SOME WILDLIFE I SAW WAS

THE BEST PART OF GRAND CANYON IS

ONE THING I WILL TELL MY FRIENDS IS

ONE THING I WILL ALWAYS REMEMBER IS

ARIZONA

GREAT BASIN national park

Established in October 1986, the park's name, Great Basin, refers to a peculiarity of drainage in the area. Here, the water of streams and rivers flows inland, rather than out to the ocean. It collects in shallow salt lakes, marshes and mudflats, and eventually evaporates in the desert air. In fact, there are more than 90 basins in the park, all separated by rugged mountain ranges running parallel to them. The park consists of 77,180 acres filled with impressive mountain peaks, lush meadows, towering forests filled with mountain mahogany, spruce, pine, and fir. You'll see sparkling streams, alpine lakes, and even a small glacier! This diverse landscape teems with wildlife from jack rabbits and mule deer to porcupines and mountain lions.

DAY I VISITED

THE WEATHER WAS

THE FIRST THING I NOTICED WAS

THE FIRST PLACE WE WENT WAS

I WAS SURPRISED TO SEE

I THOUGHT THE GLACIER WAS

THE ANIMALS I SAW WERE

THE NEATEST THING I SAW WAS

ONE THING I'LL TELL MY FRIENDS IS

NEVADA

and LEHMAN CAVES
national park

Sitting at an altitude of 6,800 feet, and extending a quarter-mile into the limestone and marble in the flank of the mountain Wheeler Peak, lies Lehman Caves. Thousands of years ago, during the Ice Age, higher water tables, slightly acidic from carbon dioxide gas, dissolved the limestone, leaving pockets. Over millennia, as the water drained slowly from the cave, it left behind large rooms filled with stalactites, stalagmites, columns, flowstones, and delicate white crystals. As you tour the cave's underground passages, you'll see a remarkably rich display of these formations.

DAY I VISITED

THE WEATHER WAS

WHEN I ENTERED THE CAVE I FELT

THE FIRST THING I NOTICED INSIDE WAS

THE COOLEST THING I SAW WAS

WHAT SURPRISED ME THE MOST WAS

ONE THING I WILL TELL MY FRIENDS IS

I WILL ALWAYS REMEMBER

I WOULD/WOULDN'T LIKE TO RETURN BECAUSE

NEVADA

PETRIFIED FOREST
national park

Established as a national park in 1962, this remarkable area contains an amazing abundance of lustrously colored petrified logs. On these 93,533 acres you'll witness an environment over 225 million years old! Early dinosaurs roamed this area and numerous fossil bones and fossil plants have been discovered here. The trees became petrified when they were buried under volcanic ash. Rich in silica, these sediments over many millennia replaced the wood until the logs were virtually turned to stone! Iron oxide and other minerals stained the silica to produce brilliant colors. While you may be tempted, don't plan on taking any of the rocks as souvenirs, as it's against the law!

DAY I VISITED _____

THE WEATHER WAS _____
_____

THE FIRST THING I SAW WAS _____
_____

WHAT SURPRISED ME MOST WAS _____
_____

ONE THING I REALLY ENJOYED WAS _____
_____

THE NEATEST THING I SAW WAS _____
_____

ONE THING I'LL TELL MY FRIENDS IS _____
_____
_____

I WILL ALWAYS REMEMBER _____
_____
_____

WHEN I LEFT THE PARK I FELT _____
_____
_____

ARIZONA

SAGUARO national forest

Established in 1994, this 91,446-acre park is named after the saguaro cactus, often referred to as the "monarch" of the Sonoran Desert. This extraordinary cactus has been protected within the park since 1933. Its imposing figure with its occasional odd human-looking shape grows incredibly slowly, taking close to 15 years to reach a height of just one foot. After around 50 years, it might reach seven feet, and at around 75 years it may sprout its first branches, or arms. Saguaros that live 150 years can reach a grand height of 50 feet and weigh as much as eight tons! While you're in the park, look at the diverse wildlife that survives here, including the majestic golden eagle!

DAY I VISITED

THE WEATHER WAS

THE FIRST THING I NOTICED WAS

THE LARGEST SAGUARO I SAW WAS

I WAS MOST AMAZED BY

THE NEATEST THING THAT HAPPENED WAS

ONE THING I'LL TELL MY FRIENDS IS

ONE THING I'LL ALWAYS REMEMBER IS

I WOULD/WOULDN'T RETURN BECAUSE

ARIZONA

ZION national park

This national park started out in 1909 as Mukuntuweap National Monument and in 1919 became Zion National Park. You'll probably view this park from the canyon, gazing up at an amazing panorama of cliffs, as well as a vast desert. If you wander the nature trails, you'll experience remarkably diverse display of plant life ranging from hanging gardens and orchards to sparse clumps of shrubs and bunchgrasses. You'll also see some of the more than 285 species of birds, mule deer, desert cottontails, desert horned lizards, and, if you're lucky, a mountain lion. The trails will lead you to beautiful rock formations, and shimmering pools, streams, and waterfalls!

DAY I VISITED

THE WEATHER WAS

THE FIRST THING I NOTICED WAS

SOME ANIMALS I GOT TO SEE WERE

I REALLY ENJOYED

THE BEST PART OF THE PARK WAS

AS I LOOKED AT THE VIEW I FELT

ONE THING I WILL TELL MY FRIENDS IS

I WILL ALWAYS REMEMBER

UTAH

DEATH VALLEY national park

Although President Herbert Hoover declared Death Valley a national monument on Feb. 11, 1933, it was not officially declared a National Park until Oct. 31, 1994. Today it's the largest park south of Alaska and is made up of 3,336,000 acres. And, with less than two inches of rainfall annually, and a record high temperature of 134°, it's one of the driest and hottest parks. Here you can see canyons, richly colored sand dunes, and rainbow-hued volcanic ash framed by remarkably eroded arches and rocks! At Devil's Golf Course you can see the intricate pinnacles of salt resulting from a lake that evaporated over 2,000 years ago. Listen carefully to hear the pings and pops of salt crystals bursting apart as the weather grows hotter!

DAY I VISITED

THE WEATHER WAS

THE FIRST THING I NOTICED WAS

I DIDN'T EXPECT TO SEE

THE COLORS OF THE PARK ARE

THE SALT PINNACLES REMINDED ME OF

MY FAVORITE PART OF DEATH VALLEY WAS

ONE THING I WILL TELL MY FRIENDS IS

I WOULD/WOULDN'T LIKE TO COME BACK BECAUSE

CALIFORNIA

JOSHUA TREE national park

Established in 1994, this park hosts two deserts, the Colorado and the Mojave, which come together and provide an amazing contrast between "high" and "low" desert. The Colorado Desert occupies the eastern part of the park. Sitting below 3,000 feet, its arid climate supports a parched and sparse environment of mostly creosote bush, a low and spindly plant that small animals use for shelter from the heat of the sun. The Mojave, or "high" desert on the western half supports the Joshua Tree, a giant member of the lily family. These tall standing yuccas serve as a focal point for wildlife, such as birds, lizards, and insects. Be on the lookout for bobcat, tarantulas, coyotes, and the roadrunner!

DAY I VISITED

THE WEATHER WAS

THE DESERT REMINDED ME OF

THE MOJAVE DESERT REMINDED ME OF

SOME ANIMALS I SAW WERE

THE MOST AMAZING THING I SAW WAS

THE NEATEST THING I DID WAS

ONE THING I WILL TELL MY FRIENDS IS

I WILL ALWAYS REMEMBER

CALIFORNIA

INYO national forest

Inyo National Forest runs 165 miles along eastern California and Nevada. It offers over 2 million acres of trees, trails, mountain peaks, and valleys. You can see twisting streams running along delicate bountiful meadows. And if you go in the spring and summer, pay a visit to Mono Lake where you'll witness the migration of what is known as the "Mono Migratory Five." Each year close to 50,000 gulls fly there to mate and lay eggs. Later, Wilson's phalaropes fly from Canada, on their way to South America. Following soon after are the red-necked phalaropes that breed near the Arctic Circle. Their arrival raises the number of phalaropes to around 150,000! Also look for around 750,000 eared grebes, and numerous snowy plovers.

DAY I VISITED

THE WEATHER WAS

THE FIRST THING I SAW WAS

IN THE FOREST, I

THE BIRDS I SAW WERE

THE PRETTIEST THING I SAW WAS

THE NEATEST THING I DID WAS

ONE THING I'LL TELL MY FRIENDS IS

I WOULD/WOULDN'T COME BACK

BECAUSE

CALIFORNIA/NEVADA 39

SEQUOIA & KINGS

Sequoia, the second oldest national park, was established in 1890 to protect the Giant Grove of Sequoias, which are known as "The Big Trees." The General Sherman Tree stands an incredible 274.9 feet high, which is as tall as a 26-story building. It is the world's largest living tree, and is between 2,300-2,700 years old. Its largest branch is almost seven feet in diameter. A year's growth of the General Sherman Tree is the equivalent to a whole new 60 foot tree! Sequoia also contains the Mineral King Valley as well as Mount Whitney, which at 14,491 feet is the highest mountain in the United States outside of Alaska.

DAY I VISITED _____

THE WEATHER WAS _____

THE FIRST THING I DID WAS _____

WHEN I SAW THE GIANT TREES I FELT _____

I REALLY ENJOYED _____

I WAS SURPRISED TO LEARN _____

SOME ANIMALS I SAW WERE _____

THE NEATEST THING I SAW WAS _____

ONE THING I WILL TELL MY FRIENDS _____

CALIFORNIA

CANYON national park

Kings Canyon, which abuts Sequoia, was established in 1940. Between the two parks, there are 1,419,075 acres, measuring 66 miles long and 36 miles at the widest point. As you hike along the hundreds of trails there are eleven peaks higher than 14,000 feet running along the eastern boundaries and providing a spectacular view of the mountains of the Great Western Divide. Cedar Grove, a breathtaking mile-deep valley, is in this sister park, along with Crystal Cave, unique in that it is formed from marble, rather than limestone. Throughout both parks you'll encounter many forms of wildlife such as coyotes, gray foxes, bobcats, and black bears.

DAY I VISITED

THE WEATHER WAS

TODAY I WENT

IN THE CAVE I SAW

I WAS SURPRISED AT

THE NEATEST THING I SAW WAS

SOME ANIMALS I SAW WERE

ONE THING I'LL ALWAYS REMEMBER IS

I WILL TELL MY FRIENDS ABOUT

CALIFORNIA

YOSEMITE

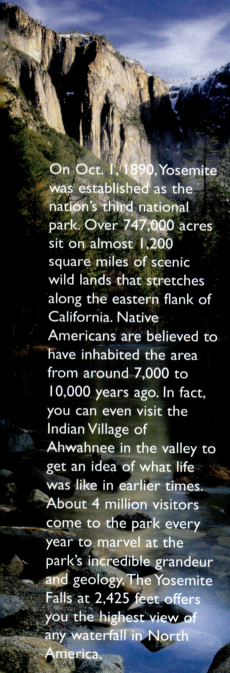

On Oct. 1, 1890, Yosemite was established as the nation's third national park. Over 747,000 acres sit on almost 1,200 square miles of scenic wild lands that stretches along the eastern flank of California. Native Americans are believed to have inhabited the area from around 7,000 to 10,000 years ago. In fact, you can even visit the Indian Village of Ahwahnee in the valley to get an idea of what life was like in earlier times. About 4 million visitors come to the park every year to marvel at the park's incredible grandeur and geology. The Yosemite Falls at 2,425 feet offers you the highest view of any waterfall in North America.

DAY I VISITED

THE WEATHER WAS

THE FIRST THING I NOTICED WAS

I DIDN'T EXPECT TO SEE

THE INDIAN VILLAGE LOOKED

SEEING YOSEMITE FALLS MADE ME FEEL

THE NEATEST THING THAT I SAW WAS

ONE THING I WILL TELL MY FRIENDS IS

SOME ANIMALS I SAW WERE

national park

If you stand at the Tunnel View Overlook, you will see one of the most photographed places in the nation. In one spectacular view you look upon El Capitan, Half Dome, Sentinel Rock, Cathedral Rocks, and the glorious Bridalveil Falls. As you head south to Mariposa Big Tree Grove, be on the lookout for the various wildlife such as California bighorn sheep and mule deer wandering around the park. Once inside the forest, you've got to see the grove's giant sequoia trees. In fact, the best known tree even has a name, the Grizzly Giant, estimated to be a whopping 2,700 years old!

DAY I VISITED

THE WEATHER WAS

THE FIRST PLACE WE WENT TODAY WAS

I WAS SURPRISED TO SEE

SEEING HALF DOME MADE ME FEEL

SOME ANIMALS I SAW WERE

MY FAVORITE PART OF YOSEMITE WAS

ONE THING I WILL TELL MY FRIENDS IS

I WOULD/WOULDN'T LIKE TO COME BACK BECAUSE

CALIFORNIA

SIERRA national forest

Set between Yosemite and Kings Canyon, these 1,303,037 acres offer a landscape of craggy peaks, rugged backcountry, giant glacial stairways, and mountainside amphitheaters filled with lakes and open meadows. You'll come across deep canyons and gorges, right within the forest! There are five wilderness areas, and one named after John Muir is filled with snowcapped peaks, dense forests, and lakes. Another, the Ansel Adams wilderness area, has one of the most dramatic mountain ranges in the United States, the jagged peaked Ritter Range. As you visit this spectacular forest, expect to see a lot of wildlife, such as deer, bears, bobcats, beavers, and coyotes.

DAY I VISITED

THE WEATHER WAS

THE FIRST THING I SAW WAS

THE MOST BREATHTAKING VIEW WAS

THE AREAS I VISITED WERE

THE MOST FUN THING I DID WAS

SOME ANIMALS I SAW WERE

THE BEST PART OF THE FOREST WAS

ONE THING I'LL ALWAYS REMEMBER IS

CALIFORNIA

BADLANDS national park

Established on Nov. 10, 1978, this unusual 244,300-acre park was home 23 million to 35 million years ago to some of the first mammals known to exist on earth. One of the world's finest Oligocene fossil beds of mammals lies here (Oligocene is a time period from the middle of the Tertiary epoch, the first geologic period of the Cenozoic Era. This is when birds and mammals first appeared). You'll see "The Wall," a hundred-mile-long stretch of tiered colorful undulating cliffs and gullies of the Badlands. Be on the lookout for wildlife such as coyotes, bison, bighorn sheep, golden eagles, and even black-footed ferrets!

DAY I VISITED

THE WEATHER WAS

THE FIRST THING I NOTICED WAS

SOME FOSSILS I SAW WERE

I WAS SURPRISED TO LEARN

I THINK GEOLOGY IS/ISN'T INTERESTING BECAUSE

THE NEATEST THING I DID WAS

LOOKING AT "THE WALL" MADE ME FEEL

I WOULD/WOULDN'T COME BACK BECAUSE

SOUTH DAKOTA

BLACK CANYON OF THE GUNNISON
national park

On Oct. 21, 1999, Black Canyon became the 55th national park in the United States, and at 30,385 acres, the third smallest. The canyon was originally over 50 miles long, but three dams have been built and have flooded two-thirds of the gorge. Of the 13 remaining miles of the canyon, one of the most scenic remains. One of the steepest and darkest parts has been eroded over time to a depth of 2,702 feet. The top of the canyon narrows to around 1,150 feet, and at the bottom it narrows at one point to about 40 feet! The rocks you see at the bottom are nearly 2 billion years old! In fact, the only time that you're able to see the bottom is when the sun finally reaches it at midday!

DAY I VISITED _____

THE WEATHER WAS _____

THE FIRST THING I DID WAS _____

WHEN I LOOKED DOWN THE GORGE I FELT _____

I WAS SURPRISED TO LEARN _____

THE NEATEST PART ABOUT THE PARK IS _____

THE BEST PART WAS WHEN _____

ONE THING I'LL TELL MY FRIENDS IS _____

I WILL ALWAYS REMEMBER _____

COLORADO

BRIDGER-TETON national forest

Bordering Grand Teton and Yellowstone, this enormous forest encompasses 3,439,809 acres, within Jackson Hole. There are three wilderness areas, several glaciers and the state's highest mountain, Gannett Peak, shared with the Shoshone National Forest. In the Bridger Wilderness area you'll find more than 1,300 lakes, Gannett Peak and 500 miles of hiking trails. The Teton Wilderness preserves in the northern section of the forest sometimes has snow on the ground as late as early July! But in this alpine area you can also see steep canyons, bountiful meadows, shimmering streams, and wondrous waterfalls!

DAY I VISITED

THE WEATHER WAS

THE FIRST THING I NOTICED WAS

THE MOST IMPRESSIVE PLACE I VISITED WAS

I REALLY ENJOYED SEEING

ONE THING THAT SURPRISED ME WAS

THE PRETTIEST PART OF THE FOREST WAS

I WILL TELL MY FRIENDS ABOUT

I WILL ALWAYS REMEMBER

WYOMING   47

GRAND TETON

The Teton mountain range began forming five million to nine million years ago along a fault line, when one part of the earth started to shift up and another one started to shift down. In recognition of its amazing beauty, Congress established Grand Teton National Park on Feb. 26, 1929. At that time, the park had about 96,000 acres. In 1943 President Franklin D. Roosevelt issued a proclamation establishing Jackson Hole National Monument, and these 210,000 acres also became part of the park. Today, there are close to 310,000 acres in this park. The highest peak of Grand Teton has an elevation of 13,770 feet, and 12 peaks are over 12,000 feet. While Grand Teton receives only about 10 inches of rain a year, it receives approximately 191 inches of snow!

DAY I VISITED

THE WEATHER WAS

THE FIRST THING I NOTICED WAS

I DIDN'T EXPECT TO SEE

WHEN I LOOKED DOWN THE CANYON, I FELT

THE MOST AMAZING THING TO ME IS

I WAS SURPRISED TO LEARN

ONE THING I'LL TELL MY FRIENDS IS

I WILL ALWAYS REMEMBER

WYOMING

national park

While you're here you can expect to see elk, moose, deer, antelope, bears, beavers, and swans! And look up in the sky where over 300 species of birds might fly. Cranes, geese, ducks, even bats will soar above! Here you can see a panoramic view of the Grand Tetons, and at the bottom of the great gulch carved from glaciers that lie beneath the north face, you can see the Teton Glacier. Make sure you look for the flat-topped Mount Moran with its Falling Ice Glacier for another spectacular view. In the park you can see over 900 species of flowering plants, shimmering streams, rushing falls, and wandering wildlife. The beauty of it all will astound you!

DAY I VISITED

THE WEATHER WAS

TODAY I GOT TO

SOME ANIMALS I GOT TO SEE WERE

THE BEST PART OF THE DAY WAS

THE BIRDS I SAW IN THE SKY WERE

THE BEST PART OF TODAY WAS

ONE THING I'LL TELL MY FRIENDS IS

I WOULD/WOULDN'T LIKE TO COME BACK BECAUSE

WYOMING 49

ROCKY MOUNTAIN

On Jan. 26, 1915, President Woodrow Wilson signed legislation creating Rocky Mountain National Park. Here, elevations range from 7,840 feet at the park headquarters to 14,255 feet at Longs Peak. In fact, 78 named peaks in the park reach an elevation of 12,000 feet and higher. As you make your way around the park, you'll also notice a marked difference in the landscape as you change elevation. At the lower levels you'll see pines, junipers, and Douglas fir. As you make your way up, you'll be greeted by meadows of wildflowers, Englemann spruce and sub-alpine fir. Higher still you'll encounter a cold, harsh alpine tundra where more than one-quarter of the plants can also be found in the Arctic!

DAY I VISITED

THE WEATHER WAS

THE FIRST THING I NOTICED WAS

THE ANIMALS I SAW WERE

THE TRAIL WE TOOK WAS

THE VIEW MADE ME FEEL

THE PRETTIEST PART OF THE PARK WAS

I WAS SURPRISED TO SEE

THE ONE THING I'LL ALWAYS REMEMBER IS

COLORADO

national park

On the 265,769 acres in this park, you'll see rolling hills, striking summits, and tiny tundra flowers. If you hike along Trail Ridge Road, you'll be following a 10,000-year-old trail that takes you higher and higher into a cold expanse similar to that in Siberia. Along the way, you might see bighorn sheep, coyotes, bobcats, and elk. You'll notice a change in the forests as well, as they turn sub-alpine filled with Englemann spruce and sub-alpine fir. You'll be amazed at the brilliant colors of the wildflowers that survive in the openings of the forests. As you hike higher you'll be able to see canyons, valleys, and meadows carved from glaciers long ago.

DAY I VISITED

THE WEATHER WAS

TODAY I WENT

I GOT THERE BY

THE ANIMALS I SAW WERE

THE MOST EXCITING THING THAT HAPPENED WAS

ONE THING THAT SURPRISED ME WAS

I WILL TELL MY FRIENDS ABOUT

I WILL ALWAYS REMEMBER

COLORADO

ROOSEVELT

Established on Nov. 10, 1978, this park pays tribute to President Theodore Roosevelt, the founder of the national park system. Located in the North Dakota Badlands, this area dates back 60 million to 65 million years! At that time the climate was subtropical, similar to present-day Florida! Back then, streams carried eroded materials from the then young Rocky Mountains, causing erosion of the area and forming the amazing cliffs, coiling gullies, and wild-looking rock formations that you see today.

DAY I VISITED

THE WEATHER WAS

THE FIRST THING I NOTICED WAS

THE FIRST PLACE I WENT WAS

THE MOST EXCITING THING THAT HAPPENED WAS

SOME ANIMALS I SAW WERE

ONE THING I WILL TELL MY FRIENDS IS

I WILL ALWAYS REMEMBER

NORTH DAKOTA

national park

Located on these 70,447 acres are over 180 species of birds, including bald and golden eagles. The park also has an amazingly dense population of wildlife. Pronghorn antelope, bull elk, bison, badgers, coyotes, bobcats, and wild horses roam throughout the park. Visit Maltese Cross Cabin, where Teddy Roosevelt spent many hours being a cowboy and later wrote his memoirs. Here you can see period furnishings and some of his personal belongings as you get an idea of what life might have been like living back in the wild wild West. Plan on taking a scenic drive to the Painted Canyon Overlook to view a magnificent colored panorama. Or head over to the north unit to see the bizarre Caprock formations.

DAY I VISITED

THE WEATHER WAS

THE FIRST THING I DID WAS

TODAY I VISITED

I GOT THERE BY

THE PRETTIEST THING I SAW WAS

THE ANIMALS I SAW WERE

THE MOST AWESOME VIEW WAS

MY FAVORITE PART OF THE VISIT WAS

NORTH DAKOTA

WATERTON/GLACIER

Waterton-Glacier is the world's first International Peace park. Established in 1932 by Canada and the United States, this park encompasses over 1,000,000 acres of wilderness filled with some of the most spectacular mountain scenery anywhere in the western United States. Over millions of years, geological processes formed and sculpted the magnificent peaks here, along with around 50 glaciers and 650 lakes. The U-shaped valleys, with rock layers billions of years old, summits, and walls, as well as most of the lakes are all the legacy of the last ice age. Although each of the parks is administered separately, the United States and Canada cooperate in maintaining the wildlife, protecting critical habitats, and conducting scientific research.

DAY I VISITED

THE WEATHER WAS

THE FIRST THING I NOTICED WAS

THE PART OF THE PARK I VISITED WAS

THE MOST BEAUTIFUL THING I SAW WAS

I WAS VERY IMPRESSED BY

THE ANIMALS I SAW WERE

ONE THING THAT I WILL TELL MY FRIENDS IS

I WILL ALWAYS REMEMBER

MONTANA/CANADA

national park

Although the park has a geologic history millions of years old, recent archaeological finds have revealed evidence of humans dating back 10,000 years! The people may have been the early ancestors of the Blackfoot, Salish, and Kootenai Indian tribes, whose many sacred sites are located throughout the general area of the park. As you visit the park, you'll discover it provides a haven for 270 species of birds, more than 1,800 types of plants, and distinct local variations of wildflowers like the glacier lily. The park is also home to 63 native species of mammals. You might see moose, minks, mountain goats, bighorn sheep, elk, otters, wolverines, and perhaps, in the distance, a herd of bison or a grizzly bear.

DAY I VISITED

THE FIRST THING I NOTICED WAS

TODAY IN THE PARK WE WENT TO

THE MOST BEAUTIFUL THING I SAW WAS

THE ANIMALS I SAW WERE

THE BEST THING THAT HAPPENED WAS

THE ONE THING I ENJOYED MOST WAS

I WILL ALWAYS REMEMBER

I WOULD/WOULDN'T COME BACK BECAUSE

MONTANA/CANADA   55

LEWIS AND CLARK
national forest

Located in west central Montana, this forest of 1,843,397 acres is divided into two districts. The Rocky Mountain Division, which lies along the eastern slope, has rugged mountain peaks that rise from the grasslands to elevations between 7,000 and 8,000 feet and hold snow for 10 months out of the year. The Jefferson Division contains scattered inland mountain ranges that dot the prairie with short dome-like peaks that have moderate slopes, and rolling hills with broad plateaus. Between the two of them, you have over 1,700 miles of trails to follow and go through two wilderness areas. Along the way you'll encounter majestic bald eagles, peregrine falcons, black bears, elk, mountain goats, and the state's largest herd of bighorn sheep.

DAY I VISITED

THE WEATHER WAS

THE FIRST THING I SAW WAS

THE FIRST PLACE I VISITED IN THE FOREST WAS

THE ANIMALS I SAW WERE

THE MOST BEAUTIFUL THING I SAW WAS

THE BEST THING I DID WAS

ONE THING I'LL TELL MY FRIENDS IS

I WILL ALWAYS REMEMBER

MONTANA

SHOSHONE national forest

Established as part of the Yellowstone Timberland Reserve by presidential proclamation in 1891, the nation's oldest national forest has over 2.4 million acres of terrain ranging from sagebrush flats to rugged mountains. Its boundaries extend south from Montana and include parts of the Beartooth, Absaroka, and Wind River Mountains. The forest includes the state's highest mountain, Gannett Peak, with an elevation of 13,804 feet! In the forest's Wapiti (elk) Valley, you'll find some of the most superlative scenery anywhere in the United States. You can see elk, deer, moose, bighorn sheep, and grizzly bears! In the Washakie Wilderness area you will find an amazing abundance of petrified wood, and in the Popo Agie Wilderness Area, more than 200 lakes!

DAY I VISITED

THE WEATHER WAS

THE FIRST THING I NOTICED WAS

THE AREAS I VISITED WERE

THE MOST BREATHTAKING THING WAS

SOME ANIMALS I SAW WERE

THE BEST PART OF THE VISIT WAS

ONE THING I'LL TELL MY FRIENDS IS

I WILL ALWAYS REMEMBER

WYOMING 57

YELLOWSTONE

Around 600,000 years ago, the center of this park erupted in a gigantic volcanic explosion. Running lava flowed for thousands of miles, and at the center remained a simmering collapsed crater approximately 28 by 47 miles. In 1872 Yellowstone was established as the world's first national park, deriving its name from the Yellowstone River. Located in the northwest corner of Wyoming and bordering Montana and Idaho, its more than 2.2 million acres on 3,472 square miles is filled with forests, meadows and wildlife. Its highest point is 11,358 feet at Eagle Peak, and the lowest is 5,282 at Reese Creek. With most of the park sitting atop a high plateau, it offers an unbelievable panorama of craggy cliffs, dazzling waterfalls, bubbling mudpots, and gushing geysers.

DAY I VISITED

THE WEATHER WAS

THE FIRST THING I NOTICED WAS

WHEN I SAW OLD FAITHFUL I

THE CLIFFS REMINDED ME OF

THE MUDPOTS WERE

THE VIEW MADE ME FEEL

ONE THING I'LL TELL MY FRIENDS IS

I WILL ALWAYS REMEMBER

58 IDAHO / MONTANA / WYOMING

national park

During your visit you'll be able to look at one of the largest gatherings of free-roaming animals in the United States. There are 290 species of birds, 58 species of mammals, and 1,050 species of native plants. Be on the look out for bison, elk, bears, coyotes, foxes, reptiles, and wolves. If you're lucky, you may see a mountain lion or some bighorn sheep. But you absolutely must visit the Geyser Basins to experience the eruption of Old Faithful. And try to make it over to Fountain Paint Pot, a bubbling cauldron of reddish-pink mud that constantly burps and belches its oozy goo. Or better yet, visit Mud Volcano and Black Dragon's Caldron, which have been known to hurl football-sized blobs of mud 10 feet!

DAY I VISITED

THE WEATHER WAS

TODAY I GOT TO

THE ANIMALS I SAW WERE

ONE THING THAT SURPRISED ME WAS

THE BEST OF TODAY WAS

ONE THING I'LL TELL MY FRIENDS IS

I WILL ALWAYS REMEMBER

I WOULD/WOULDN'T COME BACK HERE BECAUSE:

IDAHO/MONTANA/WYOMING

TARGHEE national forest

Named after a Bannock Indian peacemaker, this magnificent 1,810,000-acre forest offers you a choice of timbered highlands with peaks over 10,000 feet or lower arid semi-desert sagebrush covered land. You can hike through 1,200 miles of trails filled with rushing rivers, sparkling streams, luminescent lakes, and dazzling waterfalls. As you make your way through the forest, you should be able to spot moose, elk, antelope, mountain goats, white-tail deer as well as numerous other small animals and game birds. The park also offers activities such as a five-mile float on the first national recreation water trail, where you can see all kinds of wildlife.

DAY I VISITED

THE WEATHER WAS

THE FIRST THING I NOTICED WAS

THE FIRST THING I DID WAS

THE PLACE I VISITED IN THE FOREST WAS

SOME ANIMALS I SAW WERE

ONE ACTIVITY I DID WAS

THE BEST PART OF THE DAY WAS

I WILL ALWAYS REMEMBER

IDAHO

CRATER LAKE national park

Established on May 22, 1902, Crater Lake National Park has one of the most awe-inspiring lakes seen anywhere. Set in Mount Mazama, a dormant volcano that erupted sometime around 5,700 B.C., Crater Lake was formed when the summit collapsed and created the caldera that it now fills. As volcanic activity slowed, springs, snow and rain began to fill the caldera, resulting in the nation's deepest lake, with a depth of 1,932 feet. Rolling mountains, towering cliffs, and forests of mountain hemlock, pine, and spruce surround this scenic wonder. You'll be dazzled by the wildflowers and the abundance of bears, elk, deer, bobcats, marmot, eagles, and hawks.

DAY I VISITED

THE WEATHER WAS

WHEN I SAW CRATER LAKE I FELT

I WAS AMAZED BY

SOME ANIMALS I SAW WERE

THE NEATEST THING THAT HAPPENED WAS

THE BEST PART OF THE VISIT WAS

ONE THING I WILL TELL MY FRIENDS IS

I WILL ALWAYS REMEMBER

OREGON

LASSEN VOLCANIC
national park

Established as a national park on Aug. 9, 1916, Lassen Peak had a history of more than 150 eruptions from 1914 to early 1915, with one final small eruption in 1921. Then on May 19, 1951, the mountaintop exploded, blowing a giant mushroom cloud 7 miles into the air. The ensuing 20-foot-high wall of mud, melted snow, and ash altered the surrounding landscape. Today the park offers jagged craters, giant lava pinnacles, rugged mountains, steaming sulphur vents, and bubbling cauldrons of mud. The park serves as an excellent research tool to ecologists attempting to understand how landscapes recover from volcanic eruptions.

DAY I VISITED

THE WEATHER WAS

THE FIRST THING I NOTICED WAS

SEEING THE VOLCANO MADE ME FEEL

ONE PLACE I WENT WAS

I THOUGHT THE BUBBLING CAULDRONS WERE

THE NEATEST PART OF THE VISIT WAS

ONE THING I'LL TELL MY FRIENDS

I WILL ALWAYS REMEMBER

CALIFORNIA

LASSEN national forest

Lassen National Forest features numerous lakes formed by ancient volcanic action. Within the forest's 1,375,000 acres, you'll enjoy seeing forest fringed lakes, crater peaks, shimmering waterfalls, and majestic views of lofty mountains. In the Ishi Wilderness area, you can see bizarre pillar formations, caves, and other volcanic and glacial formations. For more excitement, at Subway Cave, you can hike through a lava tube that winds 1,300 feet through an ancient lava flow. In the Thousand Lakes Wilderness you can see mountains, ravines, open meadows, lakes, and streams. Throughout the forest you'll encounter black-tailed deer, spotted owls, black bear, elk, and pileated woodpeckers.

DAY I VISITED

THE WEATHER WAS

THE FIRST THING I SAW WAS

ONE NEAT PLACE I VISITED WAS

THE VOLCANIC FORMATIONS WERE

SOME ANIMALS I SAW WERE

THE NEATEST THING I SAW WAS

THE BEST PART OF THE DAY WAS

I WILL ALWAYS REMEMBER

CALIFORNIA 63

MOUNT RAINIER

Established on March 2, 1899, this fifth oldest national park has 235,625 acres filled with some of the most spectacular expanses of natural beauty found anywhere on earth. One hundred miles before you get to the entrance of the park, you can see the peak of Mount Rainier, the tallest peak in the Cascade Range. This volcano began to form about half a million years ago, while glaciers were carving valleys around it. In fact, these glaciers currently cover around 36 square miles of the mountain's surface. Carbon Glacier has the greatest measured thickness at 700 feet and volume at 0.2 cubic miles of any glacier in the contiguous United States.

DAY I VISITED

THE WEATHER WAS

THE FIRST THING I NOTICED WAS

THE FIRST PLACE I WENT WAS

SEEING MOUNT RAINIER MADE ME FEEL

THE GLACIERS REMINDED ME OF

THE BEST THING I DID TODAY WAS

THE ONE THING I WILL TELL MY FRIENDS IS

ONE THING I WILL ALWAYS REMEMBER IS

WASHINGTON

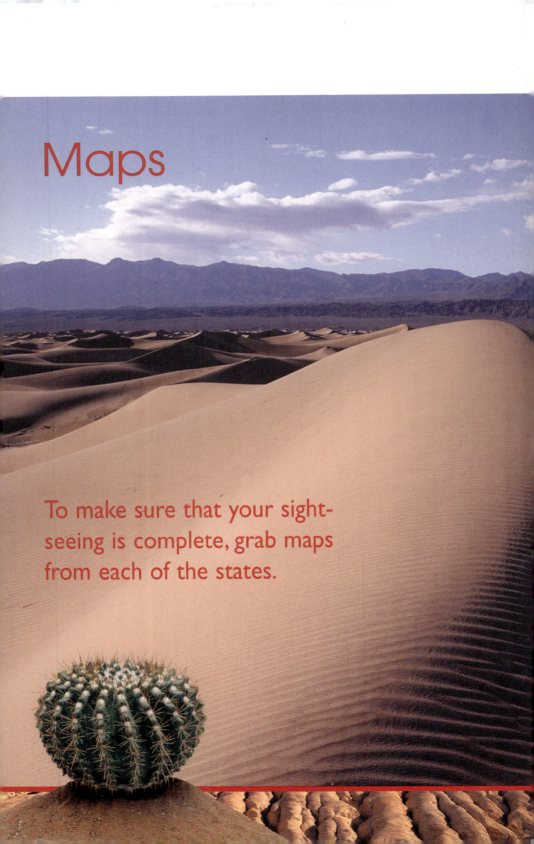

Maps

To make sure that your sightseeing is complete, grab maps from each of the states.

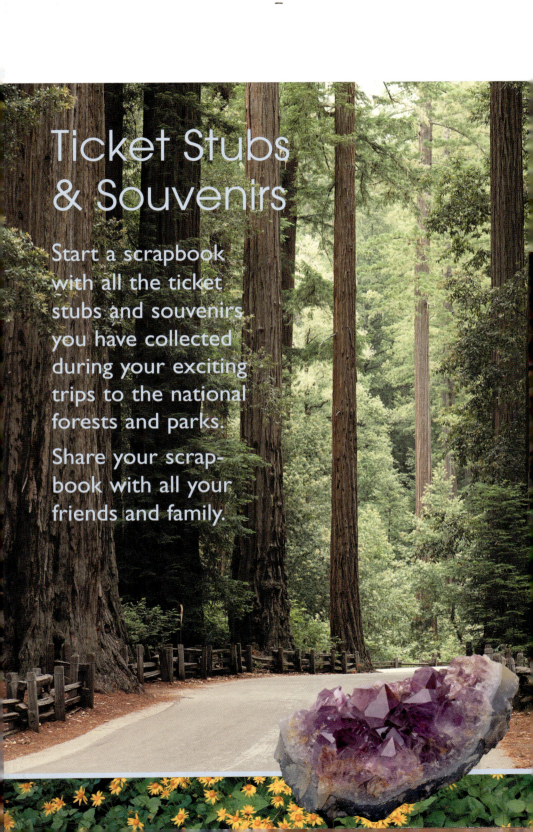

Ticket Stubs & Souvenirs

Start a scrapbook with all the ticket stubs and souvenirs you have collected during your exciting trips to the national forests and parks.

Share your scrapbook with all your friends and family.

national park

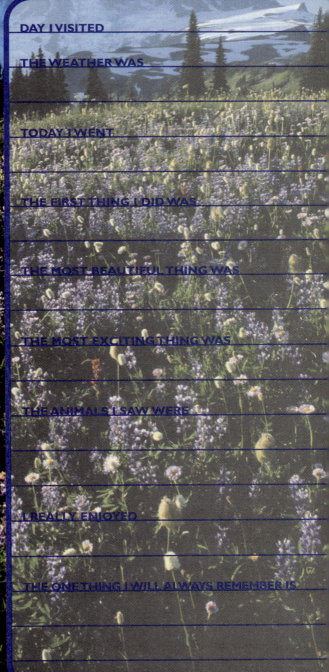

Archaeologists have discovered that five American Indian tribes lived in the area around Mount Rainier, and it appears that some people may have hunted wildlife and gathered plants and berries in the park some 2,300 to 4,500 years ago. Today, with an average of 140 inches of precipitation a year, you can find infinite fields of wildflowers, flowing waterfalls, rushing rivers, and shimmering lakes. Throughout the park you'll come across an incredible collection of wildlife, such as the hoary marmot, spotted skunk, long-tailed weasel, bobcat, cougar, mountain goat, mink, ermine, porcupine, flying squirrels, and big brown bats! Also keep your eyes peeled for the Northern saw-whet owl, chickarees, jays and nutcrackers in the sky!

DAY I VISITED

THE WEATHER WAS

TODAY I WENT

THE FIRST THING I DID WAS

THE MOST BEAUTIFUL THING WAS

THE MOST EXCITING THING WAS

THE ANIMALS I SAW WERE

I REALLY ENJOYED

THE ONE THING I WILL ALWAYS REMEMBER IS

WASHINGTON

GIFFORD PINCHOT
national forest

This spectacular forest is one of the oldest forests in the United States. There are 1,312,000 acres, with over 1,100 miles of hiking trails that contain glaciers and seven wilderness areas. Within the forest is located the Mount St. Helens National Monument, which provides a fantastic view of the volcano. You'll also find numerous lava tubes and caves formed from cooling lava. The tubes range in size from thousands of feet to small bubble-like rooms. As you visit the forest you should be able to spot a large variety of wildlife, such as elk, deer, beavers, coyote, fox, rabbits, bobcat, and if you're lucky, even the elusive cougar!

DAY I VISITED

THE WEATHER WAS

THE FIRST THING I DID WAS

THE COOLEST THING I DID WAS

IN THE FOREST I WENT TO

WHEN I SAW THE VOLCANO I FELT

I WAS MOST SURPRISED BY

SOME ANIMALS I SAW WERE

ONE THING I WILL ALWAYS REMEMBER IS

WASHINGTON

NORTH CASCADES
national park

Established by President Lyndon B. Johnson as a National Park on Oct. 2, 1968, this impressive park is often called the American Alps. Its 684,000 acres are divided into two units, North and South as one, with the Ross Lake and Lake Chelan recreational areas as the other. Within the park, you can encounter virgin forests, subalpine meadows, and hundreds of lakes and glaciers. You'll also see magnificent forests of Western hemlock, cedar and Douglas fir. On high cliffs and remote peaks you can see nimble mountain goats deftly climbing. Look closely at nearby snow-drifts and try to spot the snowshoe hare. But be on the look out for grizzly bears and cougars!

DAY I VISITED

THE WEATHER WAS

THE FIRST THING I NOTICED WAS

THE AREA WE VISITED WAS

SOME ANIMALS I SAW WERE

THE BEST THING I DID TODAY WAS

ONE THING I DIDN'T LIKE WAS

I WILL ALWAYS REMEMBER

ONE THING I WILL TELL MY FRIENDS IS

WASHINGTON

MOUNT BAKER/SNOQUALMIE
national park

This rugged forest with over 1.7 million acres offers mountains, glaciers, lakes, streams, cascading waterfalls, and both active and dormant volcanoes. Mount Baker itself is still active, and Sherman Crater still sputters and steams while releasing sulphur gases. Within the forest and its eight wilderness areas, you'll experience a diversity of landscape and climate. The lower elevations in the western edge of the forest receive only 30 to 60 inches of rain per year, but the upper elevations can receive over 500, usually in the form of snow that can be as much as 20 feet deep! Look for meadows of heather and fields of wildflowers. You'll see snowshoe hares, mountain goats, wolves, pileated woodpeckers, and the magnificent bald eagle.

DAY I VISITED

THE WEATHER WAS

THE AREA I VISITED WAS

THE FIRST THING I NOTICED WAS

THE MOST BEAUTIFUL THING I SAW WAS

SOME ANIMALS I SAW WERE

THE NEATEST THING I DID TODAY WAS

ONE THING THAT SURPRISED ME WAS

I WILL ALWAYS REMEMBER

WASHINGTON

OLYMPIC *national forest*

As you visit the 632,000 acres that comprise this forest, you will notice dramatic changes within relatively short distances. In the 50 miles between Mount Olympus and the Pacific Ocean, you can go from a lush, temperate rain forest to a lichen-filled alpine environment. Annual rainfall averages from as low as 25 inches in the southwest section known as Quilcene, with as much as 240 inches in the northeast section, known as Quinault. Many Roosevelt elk live here along with beavers, bears, and otters.

DAY I VISITED

THE WEATHER WAS

THE FIRST THING I NOTICED WAS

THE PART OF THE FOREST I VISITED WAS

I WAS SURPRISED THE MOST BY

THE NEATEST THING I DID TODAY WAS

THE MOST BEAUTIFUL THING I SAW WAS

SOME ANIMALS I GOT TO SEE WERE

I'LL ALWAYS REMEMBER

WASHINGTON

OLYMPIC

On June 29, 1938, President Franklin D. Roosevelt signed an act designating this stunning wilderness a national forest. Its 922,000 acres support three distinct ecosystems: sub-alpine forest and wildflower meadow; old growth and temperate rain forest; and miles of rugged Pacific coastline. Inside the park you'll find the Olympic mountain range crowned by 266 glaciers. Geologists believe they arose from the sea some 35 million years ago, collided with the plate supporting the North American landmass and created a dome that was sculpted by streams and glaciers into the peaks and valleys of today's Olympics.

DAY I VISITED

THE WEATHER WAS

THE FIRST THING I NOTICED WAS

THE PLACE I WENT TODAY WAS

THE NEATEST THING I SAW WAS

ONE THING THAT SURPRISED ME WAS

SOME ANIMALS I SAW WERE

THE MOST BEAUTIFUL PART OF THE PARK WAS

I WILL ALWAYS REMEMBER

WASHINGTON

national park

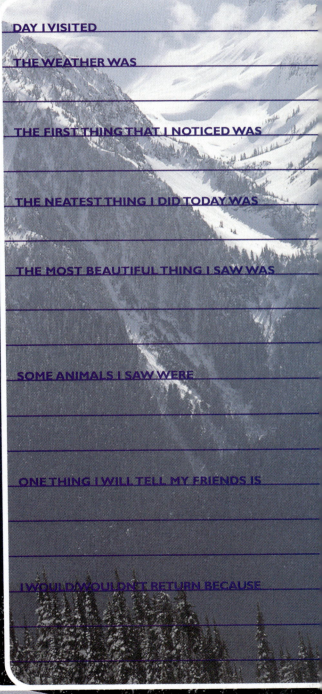
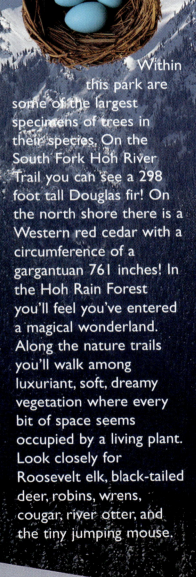

Within this park are some of the largest specimens of trees in their species. On the South Fork Hoh River Trail you can see a 298 foot tall Douglas fir! On the north shore there is a Western red cedar with a circumference of a gargantuan 761 inches! In the Hoh Rain Forest you'll feel you've entered a magical wonderland. Along the nature trails you'll walk among luxuriant, soft, dreamy vegetation where every bit of space seems occupied by a living plant. Look closely for Roosevelt elk, black-tailed deer, robins, wrens, cougar, river otter, and the tiny jumping mouse.

DAY I VISITED

THE WEATHER WAS

THE FIRST THING THAT I NOTICED WAS

THE NEATEST THING I DID TODAY WAS

THE MOST BEAUTIFUL THING I SAW WAS

SOME ANIMALS I SAW WERE

ONE THING I WILL TELL MY FRIENDS IS

I WOULD/WOULDN'T RETURN BECAUSE

WASHINGTON

REDWOOD
national park

Established Oct. 2, 1968 and expanded March 27, 1978, this national park is home to some of the world's tallest trees. Here you can see the tallest known redwood, measured in 1963 at 367.8 feet. That's about as high as a 35-story skyscraper! There are three members of the redwood family: coast redwoods; giant sequoias; and dawn redwoods. The giant sequoias can live up to 3,200 years, grow to 311 feet, with a diameter of 41 feet! As you visit the park, you'll encounter a variety of wildlife that will surprise you. Due to the diversity of the park's ecosystem, not only can you see black bears, bald eagles, and cougars, but this park is also home to pelicans, sea lions, and even gray whales!

DAY I VISITED

THE WEATHER WAS

THE AREA OF THE PARK I VISITED WAS

THE FIRST THING I NOTICED WAS

THE TALLEST TREE I SAW WAS

WHEN I SAW IT I FELT

SOME ANIMALS I SAW WERE

THE NEATEST THING THAT HAPPENED WAS

I WILL ALWAYS REMEMBER

72 CALIFORNIA

SIX RIVERS national forest

Named for the six rivers that run through it, this national forest also has six botanical areas filled with wondrous wild flowers, such as the carnivorous California pitcher plant. As the Pacific Ocean strongly affects the climate, you could easily encounter a soft blanket of misty fog when it's not snowing or raining. As you hike or horseback ride through the forest's 1,300,000 acres, you'll come across landscapes ranging from craggy mountain peaks, giant glacial stairways, to soft mountain meadows. The wildlife abounds, with bears, beavers, bobcats and coyotes. You'll also see the majestic bald eagle and the peregrine falcon.

DAY I VISITED

THE WEATHER WAS

THE PART OF THE FOREST I VISITED WAS

THE FIRST THING I DID WAS

THE THING I ENJOYED THE MOST WAS

SOME ANIMALS I SAW WERE

THE MOST BEAUTIFUL THING I SAW WAS

MY FAVORITE PART OF THE DAY WAS

I WILL ALWAYS REMEMBER

CALIFORNIA

DENALI national park

Established on Feb. 26, 1917, this park was originally called Mount McKinley National Wildlife Refuge. The park received the name Denali in 1980 and was enlarged to over 6 million acres, which is larger than the state of Massachusetts! It's one of the world's last great wilderness areas. Here you can experience displays of stunning landscape and wildlife unparalleled anywhere. Against the backdrop of massive Mount McKinley, you'll see a wondrous collection of over 650 species of flowering plants. Wandering freely are caribou, moose, grizzly bears, and wolverines. Soaring above you'll witness the regal golden eagle and hawk owls from the 156 species of birds that occupy the park.

DAY I VISITED

THE WEATHER WAS

THE FIRST THING I NOTICED WAS

SEEING MOUNT MCKINLEY MADE ME FEEL

THE ANIMALS I SAW WERE

THE MOST AMAZING THING I SAW WAS

THE BEST PART OF THE DAY WAS

ONE THING I WILL TELL MY FRIENDS IS

I WILL ALWAYS REMEMBER

ALASKA

TONGASS national forest

Nearly the size of Maine, this 17 million-acre national forest is the nation's largest. President Teddy Roosevelt created it in 1907, taking the name from the Tongass clan of Tlingit Indians that lived along the southern edge. Consisting mostly of islands, the forest also includes a mountainous mainland strip deeply cleft by fiords, bays, inlets, and channels with glaciers. The abundant wildlife includes trumpeter swans, bald eagles, and the Alaskan brown grizzly bear. One of the most interesting features of the forest is its caves, including El Capitan, a limestone cave system with 11,000 feet of mapped passages. And remarkably, grizzly bear bones at least 12,000 years old have been found inside!

DAY I VISITED

THE WEATHER WAS

THE FIRST THING I SAW WAS

THE PLACE WE VISITED WAS

I WAS SO AMAZED TO SEE

THE MOST BEAUTIFUL THING I SAW WAS

THE ANIMALS I SAW WERE

THE NEATEST THING I DID TODAY WAS

I WILL ALWAYS REMEMBER

ALASKA

75

CROSSWORD

Answers on page 50.

Across
4. These howl at the moon at night.
5. This cactus can grow 50 feet tall.
8. These trees are often giant sized.
10. Pirates used to prowl this park.
11. This park borders three states.
12. Name of a famous bear.

Down
1. These homes are also known as cliff dwellings.
2. You go spelunking in this.
3. This bird knocks on trees.
6. Mount Ranier has plenty of these.
7. Spires in Bryce Canyon are called this.
9. You might see caribou in this park.

Wacky Parks Story

Dear Diary,

   Today started out **1**_____ because I was finally going on vacation to visit some **2**_____. Since I really love nature, I couldn't wait to **3**_____ in the car and begin the trip. So we left early, but first we had to stop and have breakfast at Pretty **4**_____'s Pancake Palace. Since I'm rather daring, I thought **5**_____ pancakes would be interesting, so I ordered that covered with **6**_____. After all, I am on vacation, so anything goes. After breakfast I was feeling pretty **7**_____ so I thought I'd **8**_____ during the rest of the drive. As I looked out the window I counted the number of **9**_____ **10**_____ we passed, but I didn't see too many. We passed **11**_____. so I knew we were getting close. "**12**_____" I said, as I looked ahead in the distance and spotted some **13**_____ **14**_____. "I think we're almost there! I can see **15**_____ **16**_____!" I exclaimed **17**_____. Up above I saw **18**_____ **19**_____ in the sky. "**20**_____" I said, "they're so **21**_____. I wish **22**_____ could see this." From that moment on, I knew this trip was **23**_____ and I would always **24**_____ it.

1. adjective _____
2. plural noun _____
3. verb _____
4. person's name _____
5. fruit _____
6. plural junk food _____
7. adjective _____
8. verb _____
9. color _____
10. plural noun _____
11. city _____
12. exclamation _____
13. adjective _____
14. plural noun _____
15. adjective _____
16. plural noun _____
17. adverb _____
18. plural noun _____
19. verb ending in "ing" _____
20. exclamation _____
21. adjective _____
22. best friend _____
23. adjective _____
24. verb _____

Index

Acadia National Park, ME ... 6
Arches National Park, UT ... 20
Badlands National Park, SD ... 45
Big Bend National Park, TX ... 21
Biscayne National Park, FL ... 7
Black Canyon of the Gunnison National Park, CO ... 46
Bridger-Teton National Forest, WY ... 47
Bryce Canyon National Park, UT ... 22
Canyonlands National Park, UT ... 24
Capital Reef National Park, UT ... 25
Carlsbad Caverns National Park, NM ... 26
Chequamegon National Forest, WI ... 8
Cherokee National Forest, TN ... 9
Crater Lake National Park, OR ... 61
Daniel Boone National Forest, KY ... 16
Death Valley National Park, CA ... 37
Denali National Park, AK ... 74
Dixie National Forest, UT ... 23
Everglades National Park, FL ... 10
George Washington National Forest, VA ... 18
Gifford Pinchot National Forest, WA ... 66
Grand Canyon National Park, AZ ... 30, 31
Grand Teton National Park, WY ... 48, 49
Great Basin National Park, NV ... 32
Great Smoky Mountains National Park, NC & TN ... 11

Index

Hot Springs National Park, AR 12
Inyo National Forest, CA 39
Isle Royale National Park, MI 14
Jefferson National Forest, VA 19
Joshua Tree National Park, CA 38
Lassen National Forest, CA 63
Lassen Volcanic National Park, CA 62
Lehman Caves National Park, NV 33
Lewis & Clark National Forest, MT 56, 57
Lincoln National Forest, NM 27
Mammoth Cave National Park, KY 15
Mesa Verde National Park, CO 28
Mount Baker/Snoqualmie National Park, WA 68
Mount Ranier National Park, WA .64, 65
North Cascades National Park, WA .67
Olympic National Forest, WA 69
Olympic National Park, WA 70, 71
Ouachita National Forest, AR 13
Petrified Forest National Park, AZ 34
Redwood National Park, CA 72
Rocky Mountain National Park, CO 50, 51

Index

Roosevelt National Park, CO 52, 53
San Juan National Forest, CO 29
Saguaro National Park, AZ 35
Sequoia & Kings Canyon National Park, CA 40, 41
Shenandoah National Park, VA 17
Shoshone National Forest, WY 57
Sierra National Forest, CA 44
Six Rivers National Forest, CA 73
Targhee National Forest, ID 60
Tongass National Forest, AK 75
Waterton/Glacier National Park, Alberta,
    Canada & MT 54, 55
Yellowstone National Park, WY, ID, MT 58, 59
Yosemite National Park, CA 42, 43
Zion National Park, UT 36

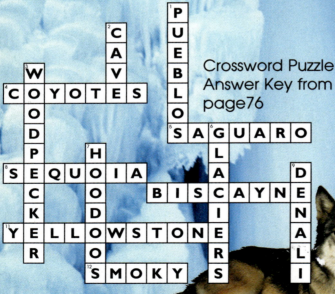

Crossword Puzzle Answer Key from page 76

80